# DREADSONG

ALISHA YASMIN

Made with ♥ on the Notion Press Platform
www.notionpress.com

# Contents

*Preface* *v*

1. Innocent Criminal 1
2. Would I Endure It? 3
3. Covered Wounds 4
4. Nameless 5
5. Dearest Heart 6
6. Hope Has Doubts 7
7. Life Will Be Perfect 8
8. Remember Me? 9
9. The Jury Of My Crimes 10
10. Villain 11
11. I Was Better Unnoticed 12
12. Not Every Story 13
13. When The Brightness Dims 14
14. Sometimes 15
15. They Say 16
16. Pain And Strife 17
17. When Your Heart Intertwines 18
18. Disagreements 19
19. The Voices 20
20. In The Depths Of Shadows 21
21. The Darkness 22
22. Another Morning 24
23. Sunset 25
24. Insufficient 26
25. Symphony 27

# Contents

About the Author 29

Final Thoughts 31

Your Thoughts, Your Journey 33

Let's Stay Connected 35

# Preface

This collection of poems is not simply a reflection of my thoughts, but rather a journey through the raw, unfiltered emotions that have shaped me. Poetry, for me, is not a craft but a way of being—a rhythm that finds me in moments of light and shadow. I don't write poems, they write me. They flow from my deepest places, sometimes without warning, taking the form of questions, frustrations, hopes, and fears.

Here, you will find verses that speak to the storms within, the quiet moments of reflection, and the unspoken truths we often hide from the world. These poems are not always neat or pretty, but they are honest. They explore the contradictions of life—the pain and joy, the love and loss, the longing and fulfillment.

As you turn these pages, I invite you to feel what is between the lines. Whether you are in the midst of your own storm or seeking solace in words, may these poems find you, just as they found me.

This is not just a book of poems; it's a collection of moments, feelings, and fragments of a journey still unfolding.

# 1. Innocent Criminal

*You've seen the smile on my face, not the tears.*
*You've seen the beauty, not the scars.*
*You knew me, but not my heart.*
*You saw me, but not my pain.*
*You tried to solve me like a* ***mystery****,*
*But you avoided the clues like they were* ***history****.*
*You said my eyes were deep,*
*And then you put tears in them.*
*You said my heart was precious,*
*That you would keep it safe,*
*And then you* ***dropped it like glass****.*
*You said I was a queen,*
*And then stole my crown.*
*You told me to trust you,*
*But never mentioned that trust included lies.*
*You bought honesty at the cost of a bunch of stories.*
*You betrayed me in a way not everyone understands.*
*You* ***stabbed me with your words****,*
*And* ***cut me in silence****.*
*When the blood dropped in the form of tears,*
*You said I was too dramatic.*
*I spent sleepless nights,*
*Endless crying,*
*Yet I never understood why I felt guilty—*

*Why I blamed myself.*
*You made me feel like the villain*
*When you committed the crime.*
*And you were,*
*My love,*
*You murdered my heart so* ***innocently****,*
*You became the innocent criminal.*

# 2. Would I Endure It?

*Would I **endure it?***
*Seeing myself for a day*
*In **third-person perspective**.*
*Could I listen to myself?*
*Would I be intimidated*
*By the depth of my voice?*
*Would I endure the sight of me?*
*Would I be bored by what I say?*
*Get a headache from listening?*
*Would I be grossed out*
***By how I behave?***
*Would I search for the nearest way out?*
*If I were you for a day,*
*I would finally know what you think.*
*Would it be,*
***"How weird is she?"***

# 3. Covered Wounds

*I wish I could express how I feel,*
*But the words seem to get* ***lost in between****.*
*It's not easy to recover*
*From* ***wounds that are hidden****.*
*I know I'm* ***indecisive,***
*A little too* ***sensitive.***
*I just don't know how to process it.*
*I feel empty inside most of the time.*
*I feel overwhelmed*
*By all the joys.*
*I feel frustrated*
***By the things that go underrated.***
*I feel so many things,*
*Asking this question since I was six:*
*Why do nice people get hurt?*
*Why am I like that?*

# 4. Nameless

*An **incredible crime**,*
*Truth buried in the earth like oil.*
*A face without a **name**,*
*A mind with no **shame**.*
*A terrible **fall**,*
*A child's **crawl**.*
*An empty **shell**,*
*A wound that **swells**.*
*My shivering lips,*
*Dissolving in the sand.*
*I'll be seeing you*
*In a red rainstorm.*

# 5. Dearest Heart

*Dearest **heart**,*
*I am falling **apart**.*
*My mind can't stop **thinking**,*
*Thoughts **rushing***
*That should be lost somewhere in between.*
*My brain tells me to pull away,*
*But you make me stay.*
*You've been hurt the **most**,*
*So raise a **toast***
*To the bleeding days and darkest nights*
*Where you did your best*
*To hold me tight.*
*I am fighting a war within,*
***Silently caving in**,*
*Wiping my tears,*
*Looking at my reflection, and crying again.*
*Your beats give me hope*
*At the very end,*
*Dancing away the **pain,***
*Waiting to feel whole **again.***

# 6. Hope Has Doubts

*Hope has doubts,*
*Like* ***pockets have holes****.*
*It doesn't know*
*The destination.*
*But when you're alone,*
*It knows*
*You'll be* ***clinging on****.*
*It knows*
*That all roads*
*Begin with one*
*Foot in front*
*Of the other.*

# 7. Life Will Be Perfect

*Life will be perfect, and I'll want to live more*
*When death comes knocking at the door.*
*Everyone will apologize for their faults,*
*And I will forgive.*
*The* ***dove will send the last message****,*
*Laying under the ground.*
*I will receive it,*
*And smile over the white roses,*
*Saying my* ***last goodbye***
*With a* ***mischievous grin on my face****.*

# 8. Remember Me?

*Remember me?*
*Among the* ***eight million*** *people,*
*Remember me?*
*The sight of my eyes,* ***once dull,***
*Full of emotions that* ***seemed null.***
*Can you recall the old conversations?*
*The ones that make you wonder—*
*How could I be the rain,*
*Pretending to be the thunder?*
*Can you visualize my eyes?*
*They hide so much,*
***Yet still cry a lot.***
*Can you remember my smile?*
*It may be ugly,*
*But it doesn't lie.*
*Do you still remember me?*
*When you look up at the stars,*
*Does it make you wonder*
*If I wasn't the star you liked?*

# 9. The Jury of My Crimes

*To the jury where my* ***crimes*** *lie,*
*I won't be able to* ***justify****.*
*I can't* ***defend myself****,*
*But I can define the* ***crime itself****.*
*I have been bleeding for long enough,*
*But I've caused a lot of wounds that are tough.*
*My* ***heart has been in prison****,*
*But* ***I won't tell you the reason****.*
*Today, with heavy eyes and a weak physique,*
*I stand before the jury to confess my crime.*
*This time, I am not willing to justify.*
*Maybe I am a criminal myself,*
*Which I accept with no shame.*

# 10. Villain

*Have you ever wondered how* ***villains are made?***
*How much pain it could cost to turn someone heartless,*
*How much blood it would take to turn someone red?*
*How could they laugh at the most crucial moments?*
*Have you ever wondered how many tears they have lost in silence?*
*We see their* ***dirty crimes,***
*But never see the* ***scars behind their eyes****.*
*We never hear their screams*
*When they* ***begged for help*** *or* ***cried for a helping hand****.*
*We stitched their mouths with a bunch of lies.*
*Is it only their fault?*
*Is it only a piece of grief?*
*Have you ever wondered about the suffering behind them?*
*Are they or* ***you the actual villain?***

# 11. I Was Better Unnoticed

*I was better* ***unnoticed,***
*When my outer shell protected me*
*From the* ***demons*** *outside.*
*I was better unnoticed,*
*In the lonely corner of a room filled with people.*
*Maybe* ***I hated loneliness,***
*But I was better when* ***I was alone.***
*I always wondered how it would be to be noticed,*
*But when they did notice,*
*They caused nothing but pain.*
*Don't get me wrong—*
*I met people with the purest hearts,*
*But the* ***betrayal,*** *the* ***pain,*** *the* ***trauma***
*Got the worst of me.*
*So I forgot to tell them apart.*
*Maybe I am not the only one who is suffering,*
*But* ***silent screams*** *are becoming intolerable.*
*All I want is for someone to see through my pain.*
*Maybe I would live better if I avoided their*
***filthy gazes*** *with no shame.*
*Maybe* ***I was better unnoticed,***
***Far from humans, in a silent place.***

# 12. Not Every Story

*Not every story ends with a **happy** ever after.*
*Not every **dark tunnel** has a **bright side** at the end.*
***Not** every river flows to the ocean.*
*Some form **islands as barriers**, leaving an incomplete story.*
*Life doesn't have to be a **fairy tale**,*
*And some stories end with a **bitter** taste.*
*Though the story may have some good phrases.*

# 13. When the Brightness Dims

*When the **brightness dims,***
*Even the most beautiful rose*
*Is identified by its **thorns.***
*No matter how much you have admired it,*
*If the brightness dims,*
*Your admiration turns into hatred.*
*A **butterfly** starts as a **caterpillar,***
*But **the caterpillar is unaware of the hatred.***
*Yet the butterfly doesn't know its own beautiful wings.*
*The **diamond is just a stone** after all,*
*And **loneliness can be just a metaphor***
***When you fly after a fall.***

# 14. Sometimes

*Sometimes I want to be the thunder in a thunderstorm,*
*Smashing and* ***destroying everything***
*Without a* ***conscience*** *to bother.*
*I wish to be the fire that will burn*
*Everything to the ground.*
*I want to be the* ***sea*** *sometimes,*
*Which can* ***devour everything*** *it encounters.*
*I just want to be a* ***form of danger***
*Whenever my anger rises.*
*I want to be destroyed in the* ***game of destruction***
*Before my eyes start to bleed.*

# 15. They Say

*They say* ***words cut deeper than a knife,***
*But how can they cut*
*When* ***silence has already formed a shield inside?***
*I am stuck in a storm—*
*A* ***storm of silence*** *and* ***words that have made me silent.***
*They said the storm's inside my head,*
*But what's inside my head isn't just a storm.*
*It's a* ***thunderstorm*** *over an ocean,*
*Wanting to destroy the land but hesitating.*
*It's the deadliest tornado of anger, pain, and suffering,*
*Which is just gaining its power*
*Until the day it releases,*
***When the will of death can't meet reality.***
*Maybe a villain is born,*
*Or how much pain does it take to be a hero?*

# 16. Pain and Strife

*Deep within the* ***human soul,***
*Lies a mystery we can't control.*
*A* ***yearning for meaning and truth,***
*A* ***quest for purpose since our youth.***
*We search for answers, near and far,*
*To who we are and what we are,*
*To why we're* ***here*** *and where* ***we'll go,***
*To what we'll* ***reap*** *and what* ***we'll sow.***
*But as we journey through this* ***life,***
*We face the* ***struggles, pain, and strife,***
*And oftentimes we lose our way,*
*And wonder why we're here to stay.*
*Yet in the* ***depths of our despair,***
*There's a* ***glimmer of hope*** *that's always there,*
*A light that* ***shines*** *within us* ***bright,***
*To guide us through the* ***darkest night.***
*For though we stumble and* ***we fall,***
*We have the strength to* ***rise up tall,***
*And find the courage to carry on,*
*And seek the truth that we've been drawn.*
*So let us embrace this inner flame,*
*And let it guide us through the rain,*
*And let us* ***live with purpose*** *and* ***grace,***
*And* ***leave a legacy for all to trace.***

# 17. When Your Heart Intertwines

*When your* ***heart intertwines*** *with the* ***yearning scream,***
*Can you think straight?*
*When all the blood has drained from your body,*
*Can you still* ***bleed to death?***
*When all your tears have been ignored for all these years,*
*Can you still cry out for help?*
*When you are empty but hide your emptiness with a bright smile,*
*Can you call yourself* ***sane?***

# 18. Disagreements

*I agreed to **disagreements** a lot,*
*To the point I fell apart.*
*Running in a **maze**, running away,*
*Till **I felt attacked**,*
*Shedding **tears** and **blood,** but*
*Never knew how to start,*
*How to cry or how to enjoy.*
***Asking this for a lifetime:***
*What do I really want,*
*Or what is it that I can call mine?*

# 19. The Voices

*The voices are* ***too loud*** *in the* ***symphony of chaos****.*

*I want to* ***scream****, but my voice is* ***under water****.*

*How can one be so* ***innocently violent****,*

*Yet their voice sounds so* ***luminescent?***

*The rain droplets on a leaf,*

*Or the tears running down your cheek,*

*Both turn red, whether at* ***sunrise*** *or* ***sunset.***

*With the* ***volatile paths to the Medusa Rath,***

*It's a matter of time until all* ***crumbles and dies****,*

*Before it all* ***starts*** *and* ***cries.***

# 20. In the Depths of Shadows

*In the* ***depths of shadows****,*
*A melody is born.*
*A first* ***cry*** *of* ***joy****,*
*A firstlaugh is torn.*
*In the depths of shadows,*
*A little strain of sunlight hits.*
*Blinding and bright it is,*
*But shadows are unknown to light.*
*Bright seems dark and frightening,*
*Comfort is what they belong to.*
*Darkness is all it takes to.*
*In the depths of shadows,*
*A melody is born—*
*A first cry of fear,*
*A* ***first laugh of dawn****.*

# 21. The Darkness

*The darkness creeps in,*
*A **cloak of shadows**, so **thick** and **grim**.*
*It **steals away the light,***
*And **fills my heart with fright**.*
*The world around me **fades,***
*As the night begins to **cascade.***
*The whispers of the wind,*
*Are the only sound my heart can find.*
*The **darkness envelopes** me,*
*A **shroud** that won't let me be.*
*It swallows up my soul,*
*And leaves me feeling so **alone**.*
*The **demons in my mind**,*
*Are free to **roam** and **unwind**.*
*They **twist** and **turn** in a **vicious dance**,*
*And take me down in a **cruel trance**.*
*I'm **lost in the abyss**,*
*Of a **darkness** that won't dismiss.*
*It holds me in its grip, and I fear,*
*I'll **never escape** this trip.*
*But still, I hold on,*
*To a glimmer of light, a hope that's **strong**.*
*I know that **dawn will come,***
*And with it, a **new day**, a **new song**.*

*So I'll wait and hold my* ***breath,***
*Until the darkness meets its* ***death.***
*And* ***I'll step into the light,***
*Knowing I made it through the* ***darkest night.***

# 22. Another Morning

*Morning* ***feels different*** *today.*
***Lying here****, thinking about* ***life****,*
*The* ***rising sunlight*** *is coming through the* ***closed windows****,*
*Giving me the hope I need.*
*But I'm still* ***feeling empty*** *inside.*
*The* ***twittering of the birds*** *reminds you that you haven't actually* ***escaped reality****.*
*The* ***silence of the morning feels like you're loved but lonely****.*
*It also makes you realize that somehow you've lost yourself in the process of learning about life.*
*The* ***morning breeze calms*** *you by showing you the disturbance.*
*The* ***foggy*** *nature seems like a mixture of our imagination and reality.*
*This morning, I don't have any hopes or motivation,*
*But I still can feel the* ***warmth of love*** *and the* ***loneliness*** *I've been craving.*
*I can feel the need to face the reality I've been escaping with my imagination.*
*I know it will hurt me,*
*But how far can I run away from it?*

# 23. Sunset

*It seems to be the end of another day*
*With another* ***sunset****.*
*I watched* ***the sun disappear into the horizon****,*
*The sky bidding farewell with thousands of colors.*
*It always seems like the sun's work is done,*
*And it goes to sleep*
*With so many* ***unanswered*** *questions.*
*I wonder every day, what it wants to say.*
*I long for the* ***endless horizon****,*
*Somewhere between* ***heaven and earth****.*
*Sunset signifies the* ***ending****, the* ***change****, the* ***transformation****,*
*But it gives me a deeper sense of gratitude for the earth.*
*The sunset sets hope for another day,*
*Another* ***sunrise,***
*And the same me, with* ***renewed energy****.*

# 24. Insufficient

*I still feel I have to* ***run faster****,*
*Laugh* ***louder****.*
*The sky above my head turns* ***gray****,*
*Yet I still feel so* ***blue****.*
*Even after all that, I still feel not good enough.*
*Not good enough to* ***love*** *or* ***to be loved****.*
*They tell you to try,*
*But how long, or how much, can one try?*
*And after all that, I still feel not good enough.*
*The world's running so fast,*
*And I get out of breath so* ***easily****, so* ***quickly****.*
*Yet again,* ***I feel not enough****.*

# 25. Symphony

***I don't write poems,***

***Poems write me.***

*I don't need some heart-wrenching pain*

*Or **evermore** happiness.*

***It comes to me.***

***Love me or hate me,***

***It writes me.***

*Intertwining thoughts or a blank mind,*

***Poem** finds me in every situation, despite the time bind.*

*It's as **natural** as my breath,*

*It's as **crucial** as the pain.*

*It's as **enjoyable** as the light of day,*

*It's as **miserable** as the darkness of night.*

*But it is **me** and I am **poem**,*

*With the symphony of **rhymes**.*

# About The Author

Alisha Yasmin is a writer whose heart finds rhythm in the movement of words. Drawing inspiration from the quiet, often overlooked moments of life, Alisa crafts poems that explore themes of internal conflict, emotional vulnerability, and the complex beauty of human experience. Through writing, they seek to create an intimate connection between reader and poet, a shared understanding that we are never alone in our thoughts or feelings.

# Final Thoughts

In the end, every poem is a reflection of the soul that wrote it. As you turn the final page, know that these words are not just mine—they are yours now, too. They belong to the hearts that connect with them, to the minds that ponder them. Let them be a reminder that pain, joy, confusion, and clarity can all exist in the same space—and that's okay.

Thank you for taking this journey with me.

# Your Thoughts, Your Journey

As you've traveled through these words, what thoughts, feelings, or memories have surfaced? Take a moment to write down your reflections, thoughts, or anything the poems may have stirred within you. This is your space—let your journey continue here.

# Let's Stay Connected

Thank you for reading. If you'd like to share your thoughts or ask questions, feel free to connect with me on:

- Instagram: @asthewayiam
- Twitter: @asthewayiam_
- Substack: @alishayasmin

I'd love to hear from you!

www.ingramcontent.com/pod-product-compliance
Lightning Source LLC
LaVergne TN
LVHW041300150826
845673LV00008B/2663

* 9 7 9 8 8 9 5 5 6 7 1 2 8 *